Alice in Pastaland

A Math Adventure

By *Alexandra Wright*

Illustrated by *Reagan Word*

Charlesbridge

To my parents and brother Spencer, who make it all add up — *A.W.*

To my parents, for a lifetime of encouragement — *R.W.*

Also available from Charlesbridge:
Pasta Math, by Mary Chandler, a book
of activities using pasta as manipulatives
to teach and reinforce math concepts.

Published by Charlesbridge
85 Main Street, Watertown, MA 02472
(617) 926-0329
www.charlesbridge.com

Library of Congress Cataloging-in-Publication Data
Wright, Alexandra.
    Alice in Pastaland : a math adventure / by Alexandra Wright ; illustrated
by Reagan Word.
        p. cm.
    Summary : An imaginary trip through Pastaland provides Alice with
opportunities to explore number concepts and basic arithmetic as she tries
to help a white rabbit solve a math problem.
    ISBN-13: 978-1-57091-151-4; ISBN-10: 1-57091-151-7 (softcover)
    [1. Arithmetic—Fiction. 2. Characters in literature—Fiction.
3. Pasta products—Fiction.] I. Word, Reagan, ill. II. Title.
PZ7.W9195A1 1997
[Fic]—dc21   97-5821

Printed and bound November 2009 by Sung In Printing
in Gunpo-Si, Kyonggi-Do, Korea
10 9 8 7

132\250

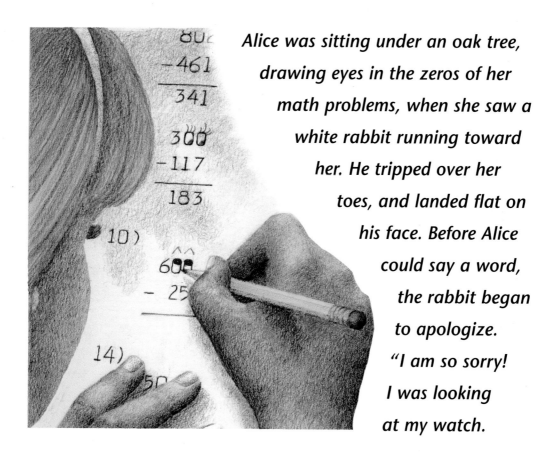

Alice was sitting under an oak tree, drawing eyes in the zeros of her math problems, when she saw a white rabbit running toward her. He tripped over her toes, and landed flat on his face. Before Alice could say a word, the rabbit began to apologize. "I am so sorry! I was looking at my watch.

"Four o'clock. I've got only an hour and a half to make pasta for 40 guests. I need one-quarter pound of pasta for each guest. No time to think how much to buy, I'm late, I'm late, I'm late!" and off he ran.

Alice was astonished to hear a rabbit speaking about math. She jumped up explaining, "You just have to multiply . . . " but he disappeared into a rabbit hole. Alice stuck her head in the hole and tried to see into the darkness. She only succeeded in losing her balance and falling . . . down . . . down . . . down.

3

Kerplunk! Alice landed with a thud. She found herself in a strange room wearing a strange dress. On a table there was a bowl of macaroni and a small key on a red ribbon. Alice looked around and saw a tiny door with a tiny keyhole. When she unlocked the door, she saw the most beautiful little garden, but the door was too small to go through.

There was a sign in the macaroni that said, "EAT YOUR PASTA." Alice wondered if she should eat it. Her mother had always told her not to take food from strangers, and Alice couldn't think of anything stranger than falling down a rabbit hole. Can you?

The macaroni smelled so good, Alice tasted it. Soon, she had eaten every single bite.

1 + 1 + 1 + 1 + 1 + 1 = 6   2 + 2 + 2 = 6   1 + 2 + 3 = 6   3 + 3 = 6

1 + 1 + 4 = 6

2 + 3 + 1 = 6

5 + 1 = 6

4 + 2 = 6

6 + 0 = 6

6 = 2 + 2 + 1 + 1

6 = 2 + 1 + 1 + 1 + 1

6 = 1 + 1 + 2 + 1 + 1

6 = 1 + 1 + 1 + 1 + 1 + 1   6 = 2 + 2 + 2   6 = 3 + 3   6 = 4 + 2   6 = 5 + 1

Something very peculiar began to happen. Was the room getting bigger? No, Alice was getting smaller! Soon, she was only eight inches high. She wondered how her little kitten, Noodles, would like it now that they were the same size. Alice realized that now she could fit through the tiny door, but when she tried to open it, it was locked. The key was back on the table, out of reach.

Frustrated, Alice sat down right next to a tiny bowl of alphabet noodles. A sign said Eat 6 Letters. Hoping that it might change her size again, Alice ate a T, an A, two L's, an E, and an R. Quickly, she began to grow until she was six feet tall! Now she could reach the key, but she was too big to get through the door. Alice was so upset, she began to cry.

Suddenly, she was swept off her feet in a salt-water wave of her own tears. "Oh no! I've shrunk again!" Alice gurgled. Spotting some animals on a beach, she swam to them. The creatures were drawing 2's in the sand and thinking of ways to get dry.

A Toucan spoke up, "I suggest a pasta race!" The Tuatara and the Cockatoo jumped up, ready to begin. "If you please, sir," Alice said to the Toucan, "what is a pasta race?"

"Well," he replied, "the best way to find out is to join in!" So she ran with the others, around in a circle. Alice thought, "There is no starting line and no finish line. Are there any rules at all?"

After 2 minutes, the Toucan shouted, "The race is over!" They all crowded around asking who had won. It seemed that everyone had won a prize pasta necklace. Alice, feeling hungry, ate hers. The other runners gasped at her bad taste. Alice tried to apologize, but they all scurried off leaving her alone on the beach.

Just then, a Walrus and a Fisherman came strolling
down the shore.

"Tell me, dear friend, Walrus, why have you been so sad?
We have plenty of seashells and our business isn't bad.
For just five cents the small ones,
And for twenty cents, the large;
It will be no time at all
'Fore we can buy a barge."

The walrus replied, sadly,
"I cry for the sweet creatures whose shells lie on the beach
While counting and collecting all of those within my reach.
I wish I'd had a lesson
So that I'd know how to teach
The little dears to add themselves
And write the price for each."

The Walrus and the Fisherman spotted Alice and asked if she would help them gather shells. "I'd be happy to help you," said Alice, "as soon as I find the White Rabbit. Have you seen him?" They thought for a long while and remembered.

"We sold the white rabbit ten dozen small shells for the Queen's party just an hour ago," said the Walrus.

"How many pounds does that weigh?" asked Alice.

"A dozen weighs one-half pound," said the Fisherman, "so ten dozen weigh five pounds."

"Oh, no! Then he didn't buy enough," said Alice. "Which way did he go?" The Walrus and the Fisherman tried to remember. "Never mind," said Alice. "I'll try this path. Thank you for your help." Then off she ran.

Alice came upon a garden of giant flowers. She wondered if the flowers were really large or if she had somehow shrunk again. Hearing voices, Alice looked around and found a group of flowers arguing.

A foxglove flower said, "I'm the biggest and the best because I grow ten spaghetti tall!"

"But most of your flowers grow down low!" a daffodil scoffed. "I grow all my flowers seven spaghetti high!"

"Height doesn't matter," a tulip said. "My flowers grow bigger than yours."

"Well," said a pansy, "I grow twice as many flowers."

Alice couldn't help remarking about her unusual growing habits lately. "I'm sure I have done more growing than any of you."

The flowers turned and stared at the intruder. "Exactly what kind of flower are you, my dear?" an iris asked. "Where are her roots?" whispered a lily. "What droopy petals," added a snapdragon.

"Oh, I'm not a flower at all. I'm a human being and I used to be 48 inches tall until I shrunk to eight inches, and then I grew to six feet tall, and . . . "

"Enough," said a tulip. "I haven't heard such nonsense since the dandelion blew by. You must be a weed!" With that, all the flowers began to shout, and Alice thought it best to leave. She hurried out of the garden and down the path.

12 + 12 + 12 + 12 + 12 + 12 = 72 12 + 12 + 12 + 12 + 12 + 12 = 72

12 + 12 + 12 + 12 = 48

12 + 12 + 12 + 12 = 48

12 + 12 + 12 + 12 = 48

12 + 12 + 12 + 12 = 48

12 + 12 + 12 + 12 = 48

12 + 12 + 12 + 12 = 48

12 + 12 + 12 + 12 = 48

12 + 12 + 12 + 12 + 12 + 12 = 72 12 + 12 + 12 + 12 + 12 + 12 = 72

Alice looked around wondering which way to go. "Why not enjoy the pastabilities here?" said a strange voice. "Thank you," said Alice, thinking it best to be polite even though she saw no one. "Here I am, up in the tree," said the Quantum Cat.

"Could you please tell me if you have seen a White Rabbit pass by?" Alice asked. The Cat replied,

"If one did, I should have.

If one were, I would have.

But as it is, I couldn't have."

Then it promptly faded away, leaving nothing but a smile and the numbers on its license tag, which added up to nine on each side. Alice carefully took nine steps, in case this was a clue.

It was. The Cat appeared in front of her, walking backward, and said, "This way will lead you to the house of the Math Hatter." Then the Quantum Cat vanished completely.

Alice walked until she found herself at the house of the Math Hatter. "Hello, my dear. Come in, do. Would you like some sauce?" he sputtered.

Before Alice could say a word, the Math Hatter wound a strand of spaghetti around her forehead and measured it onto a piece of paper. Quickly, he cut and folded a hat for her, just like his own, and invited her to decorate it.

Alice made a colorful zig-zag around the hat and put it on.

Wonderful aromas arose from the foods on the table.

In the salad bowl, the leaves of lettuce rustled and
a small snake poked its head out from behind a cucumber.

It said sleepily,
"One and one are two,
two and two are four,
four and four are eight. . ."

Alice slowly backed away from the table.

"Hold your horses, Alice," said the Math Hatter.
"Don't worry about him. That's just our little friend
the Adder."

1 + 1 = 2   2 + 2 = 4   4 + 4 = 8   8 + 8 = 16   16 + 16 = 32

1 + 1 = 2   2 + 2 = 4   4 + 4 = 8   8 + 8 = 16   16 + 16 = 32

32 + 32 = 64 16 + 16 = 32 8 + 8 = 16 4 + 4 = 8 2 + 2 = 4 1 + 1 = 2

1 + 1 = 2 2 + 2 = 4 4 + 4 = 8 8 + 8 = 16 16 + 16 = 32 32 + 32 = 64

2 + 9 + 4 = 15   7 + 5 + 3 = 15   6 + 1 + 8 = 15   8 + 3 + 4 = 15

2 + 9 + 4 = 15   7 + 5 + 3 = 15   6 + 1 + 8 = 15   8 + 3 + 4 = 15

4 + 9 + 2 = 15
3 + 5 + 7 = 15
8 + 1 + 6 = 15
4 + 3 + 8 = 15

4 + 9 + 2 = 15
3 + 5 + 7 = 15
8 + 1 + 6 = 15
4 + 3 + 8 = 15

The Adder yawned, "Do you like our math-terpiece?"

"He means our masterpiece of a centerpiece," said the March Mare.

Alice admired the plate of ravioli in the center of the table. Stenciled on each piece with pasta sauce was a number.

The Math Hatter explained, "Add the numbers any way you please, up, down, or diagonally, and you will get the same number every time. Clever, isn't it?"

Alice had just finished adding the numbers 16 different ways when the White Rabbit ran by. After explaining why she had to leave, she ran after him.

Alice ran until she came to the courtyard of a palace. She stopped to admire a large white rotini bush surrounded by three busy gardeners. Alice had never seen gardeners like these. They were pasta playing-cards. "Excuse me," Alice began, "why are you painting the rotini?"

"Well," the Five whispered, looking around nervously, "the Queen wanted a red rotini bush, but we planted a white one by mistake."

"If we don't get it painted before she finds out," the Two squeaked, "we'll be in hot water!"

Hearing the sound of a trumpet, the Five cried, "The Queen!" and the gardeners tried to hide their brushes.

The Queen roared, "What is the meaning of this white rotini?" The gardeners began bowing and explaining, but the Queen just screamed, "Off with their heads!"

Turning to Alice, the Queen demanded to know who she was. Alice replied as politely as she could, hoping the Queen would not want any more heads cut off.

"Do you like games, dear?" the Queen asked kindly. When Alice replied that she did, the Queen invited her to join in a royal game of musical chairs.

They played the game by marching around a dinner table set with 40 plates. Alice counted 10 serving bowls of different kinds of pasta. "Well, I guess the White Rabbit cooked enough," Alice thought.

While they marched around the table, a quartet played "She'll Be Coming 'Round the Pasta When She Comes."

When the music stopped, everyone scurried to sit in a chair. If players got in the Queen's way, she shouted, "Off with their heads!" Each time the music played, five chairs were taken away. Alice knew that it was only a matter of time before her head was in danger.

40 − 5 = 35   35 − 5 = 30   20 − 5 = 15   15 − 5 = 10

40 − 5 = 35   35 − 5 = 30   30 − 5 = 25   25 − 5 = 20   20 − 5 = 15   15 − 5 = 10

40 − 5 = 35   35 − 5 = 30   30 − 5 = 25   25 − 5 = 20   20 − 5 = 15

All at once, there was a great commotion. The Queen's pasta crown had been stolen! The Queen threatened to have everyone's head chopped off. The King called for a trial.

The Toucan was in charge of questioning the witnesses, and the questions were quite odd, indeed. He asked, "If a toucan adds two and two-can the answer be four?" Before the witness could reply the Toucan demanded, "What would four plus five equal, if seven ate nine?"

Suddenly, Alice realized that she was growing again. "How inconvenient," she thought. Then Alice was called as a witness. She stood up and hit her head on the ceiling. Everyone stared at her. "She stole the crown!" someone yelled. The Queen shouted, "Off with her head!"

50 52 54 56 58 60 62 64 66 68 70 72 74 76 78 80 82 84 86 88

Alice turned and ran, and the pack of playing-cards chased after her.

At the edge of the garden, White Rabbit waved to her. She ran toward him, hearing the strangely loud ticking of his watch.

With the cards at her heels, Alice realized that the White Rabbit was holding the garden gate open for her.

She ran down the path, through the gate, and floated . . . up . . . up . . . and away.

Alice flew out of the rabbit hole and landed with a
bump on soft grass. She looked around to find that she
was back where she started, under the oak tree.

Her math homework was all done and she heard
her parents calling her, "Alice, six o'clock, time for dinner.
It's your favorite."

Alice got up, smiling, "I had a feeling we'd have pasta."

15. If one person eats 1/4 pound of pasta, how
much pasta will 40 people eat? ___10 pounds___

$\text{☻} = \frac{1}{4}$ pound

$\text{☻☻☻☻} = 1$ pound

40 people = 10 groups of 4

10 groups × 1 pound = 10 pounds